Time Management

Increase Productivity and Organize Your Day with these Easy to Use Time Management Hacks!

Introduction

I want to thank you and congratulate you for purchasing the book, *Time Management: Increase Productivity and Organize Your Day with these Easy to Use Time Management Hacks!*

This book contains proven steps and strategies on how to become an effective time manager.

This book will teach you the basics of time management. It will explain how you can manage your time effectively. In addition, it will help you boost your overall productivity. This reading material contains tricks, techniques, and detailed processes related to improving your time management skills.

Here are the things you'll learn:
- The effects of psychology on time management
- How to incorporate your values into your schedule
- How to plan your schedules
- How to use charts in managing your time
- How to create a to-do list
- How to identify and prioritize tasks
- The benefits you can get from "single handling"

- How to fight procrastination
- How to control interruptions
- How to keep your telephone under control
- How to plan a meeting
- How to read quickly
- The effects of clean workspace on your productivity and time management system

Simply put, this material will arm you with thirteen-time management hacks. That means you will have thirteen techniques that you can use to manage your time well. You might think that these hacks are overly simple. Well, they may be easy to understand and implement. However, don't be fooled by their apparent simplicity. They have helped countless people in overcoming procrastination and setting up effective time management systems.

If you are looking for a quick yet comprehensive guide regarding time management, this is the book you need.

Thanks again for purchasing this book, I hope you enjoy it!

☐ **Copyright 2016 by Spirit Publishing- All rights reserved.**

This document is geared towards providing exact and reliable information in regards to the topic and issue covered. The publication is sold with the idea that the publisher is not required to render accounting, officially permitted, or otherwise, qualified services. If advice is necessary, legal or professional, a practiced individual in the profession should be ordered.

- From a Declaration of Principles which was accepted and approved equally by a Committee of the American Bar Association and a Committee of Publishers and Associations.

In no way is it legal to reproduce, duplicate, or transmit any part of this document in either electronic means or in printed format. Recording of this publication is strictly prohibited and any storage of this document is not allowed unless with written permission from the publisher. All rights reserved.

The information provided herein is stated to be truthful and consistent, in that any liability, in terms of inattention or otherwise, by any usage or abuse of any policies, processes, or directions contained within is the solitary and utter responsibility of the recipient reader. Under no circumstances will any legal responsibility or blame be held against the publisher for any reparation, damages, or monetary loss due to the information herein, either directly or indirectly.

Respective authors own all copyrights not held by the publisher.

The information herein is offered for informational purposes solely, and is universal as so. The presentation of the information is without contract or any type of guarantee assurance.

The trademarks that are used are without any consent, and the publication of the trademark is without permission or backing by the trademark owner. All trademarks and brands within this book are for clarifying purposes only and are the owned by the owners themselves, not affiliated with this document.

Table Of Contents

Introduction i

Chapter 1: Time Management – The Basics 1

Chapter 2: First Hack - Understand the Psychology Behind Time Management 4

Chapter 3: Second Hack – Improve Your Productivity by Identifying Your Personal Values... 8

Chapter 4: Third Hack – Write Down Your Plans...................... 11

Chapter 5: Fourth Hack – Utilize Charts 14

Chapter 6: Fifth Hack – Create To-Do Lists............................... 18

Chapter 7: Sixth Hack – Identify the Tasks That You Need to Do Now 21

Chapter 8: Seventh Hack – Practice "Single Handling" 25

Chapter 9: Eighth Hack – Beat Procrastination 28

Chapter 10: Ninth Hack – Manage Interruptions 31

Chapter 11: Tenth Hack - Control the Phone 34

Chapter 12: Eleventh Hack – Plan Your Meetings Well............. 36

Chapter 13: Twelfth Hack – Learn How to Read Fast................ 38

Chapter 14: Thirteenth Hack – Keep Your Workspace Organized 41

Conclusion 43

Chapter 1: Time Management – The Basics

A person's ability to manage his time, just like any important skill related to his career, can decide whether he will succeed as a professional or not. Time is an irreplaceable resource that can help you achieve your dreams. Consider it as a crucial asset that you cannot hoard or recover. You need to spend time on everything you do: you will gain excellent rewards if you can accomplish a lot of things within the time available to you.

Time management plays a critical role in reaching excellent productivity and health. If you can manage your time well, you will have a high level of harmony with other people, inner peace, and psychological wellbeing. As you probably know, people who cannot manage their time often become anxious, stressed, and/or depressed. By managing the important aspects of your life well, you will achieve greater energy and better productivity.

This book will arm you with time management hacks. By mastering the tricks, ideas, and strategies in this book, you will be able to secure at least three productive hours every day and experience an improvement in your overall effectiveness.

The hacks you'll find in this material have helped countless people. It can help you too, if you have the following:

Critical Elements of Time Management
- Desire – It is imperative that you have an intense desire to control your time and achieve an improvement in your productivity.
- Decisiveness – This characteristic plays an important role in your success: you have to make a firm decision to practice your time management skills until they turn into habits.
- Determination – Becoming an effective time manager involves various challenges. You will also face temptations to forget about what you are trying to do and just go back to your old ways. Without determination, your chances of acquiring the necessary time management skills are close to zero.
- Discipline –Experienced time managers consider this as the most important characteristic. You must have enough discipline to treat time management as an enduring practice. You should be willing to pay the price, do what is right, and perform activities in the right time, regardless of whether or not it benefits you in the short-term.

The benefits of managing your time well is tremendous. Being perceived as a great performer is just one of the "pros". Poor time management, on the other hand, often leads to bad performance.

This book will provide you with thirteen hacks that can help you bring your time management skills to the next level.

Important Note: You can't separate time management from life management. To become an effective time manager, you should value each minute of your life.

Chapter 2: First Hack - Understand the Psychology Behind Time Management

In this chapter, you'll learn the psychological basis of time management. With this hack, you will know how your brain affects the way you manage your time. Read this material carefully: if you know the psychology behind time management, you will have excellent chances of mastering the latter.

Your life's quality largely depends on how you think about yourself. Your self-esteem serves as the foundation of your personality. It dictates how you utilize your time and your life in reaching your goals. If you are efficient in using your time, you will be more confident in yourself. Having more confidence in yourself allows you to become a better time manager. As you can see, self-esteem and time management forms a self-reinforcing loop.

The Importance of Control
The "Principle of Control" serves as the core of great time management. Basically, this principle states that your self-esteem depends on your perceived control over your life. If you think you are just going with the flow, your self-esteem will plummet. If you think that

you are living your life the way you want to, on the other hand, your self-esteem will soar.

There are two types of control: internal and external. If your life relies on internal control, you feel that you have complete control over your destiny. If your life depends on external control, however, external circumstances (which you can never control) decide how you will end up.

With external control, you think that your bills, your boss, your obligations, and the pressure caused by your job dictates your life. You feel that you need to do countless things within a short period of time. In most cases, you will just react to things that are outside of your control.

Remember that action and reaction are two different things. The former lets you become a master; the latter forces you to become a slave. Performing actions help you feel positive; reacting to external stimuli makes you feel negative. Obviously, you will only become productive if you feel in control of your personal and professional lives.

How to Enhance Your Productivity and Time Management Skills

You need to change the "inside" before you can change the "outside". Visible changes result from invisible ones. If you want to experience noticeable improvements in your time management skills and overall productivity, you must feel positive about yourself first. Obviously, becoming productive is extremely difficult if you are depressed.

In this part of the book, you'll learn four techniques that you can use to improve your mindset. Once your thoughts and beliefs about yourself become positive, attaining improvements in your skills and productivity will be way much easier.

Here are the techniques that you should use:

- Decide –This is the first step of the process. You must decide to develop better time management skills. Once you have made a clear decision, the remaining parts of the process become easy and simple.
- Set Your Mind – According to psychologists, your inner dialogue (i.e. the way you converse with yourself) determine 95% of all of your actions and emotions. That means you need to

motivate yourself through positive statements. For example, you may say "I am productive and well organized" every morning and whenever you feel stressed about your work.

Your subconscious mind takes this statement as a command. Thus, your brain forces you to become the person you claim you are.

- Visualize – In most cases, words are not enough to change the way you feel about yourself. You also need to use visualization skills to improve your chances of succeeding. Imagine yourself as a relaxed, calm, efficient, and confident person.

  By visualizing the ideal version of yourself, you'll be able to exert greater control over your time.

- Act According to Your Beliefs –After telling and visualizing yourself as an effective time manager, you need to act accordingly. Visions are stronger than words, but actions are way stronger than visions. Acting as if you are already a great time manager boosts your self-esteem and your overall productivity.

Chapter 3: Second Hack – Improve Your Productivity by Identifying Your Personal Values

Because time management and life management are inseparable, improving your productivity starts with determining your own values. Keep in mind that managing time properly is impossible if you don't know the things you value.

Excellent time management involves harmonizing a set of events that you consider as top priority. If you think an activity is low priority, you won't exert any effort to manage your time well in doing it.

Answer this simple question: "Why are you doing what you are doing?"

The Purpose and Meaning of Your Life
Everyone needs a purpose and meaning. Actually, people become sad and anxious if they feel that their activities are irrelevant to their own values and beliefs. If you know the "why" behind your activities, you'll know the "when", "what", and "how" of improving your productivity.

Improving your time management skills is useless if you think that you are doing unimportant things. If you will be good at doing things that are in contrast to what you value in life, you will just become more anxious and frustrated.

The Most Important Things in Your Life
After determining your life's purpose and meaning, you must identify the things you consider as extremely important. What are the things you would stand for regardless of the situation? What are the things you would never do?

Your day-to-day activities should match your personal values. According to recent studies, poor time management results from the difference between a person's inner convictions and the things he/she needs to do.

The Techniques
Here are the techniques that you should use to incorporate your values into your time management efforts:

<u>*Believe That You Are Special*</u>
Each person is unique in terms of values. No two people have the exact set of things they consider as important. Values form an

important part of your identity. They rarely change as you grow old.

You must find your real values, and manage your time so that you are working (and living) according to those values.

Perform Self-Analysis
The following questions will help you understand your values. Once you have determined those values, use them as the basis for preparing your schedule.
- How would you describe yourself to a stranger?
- "If an alien asks you to describe humans, what would you say?" – This question will help you understand your thoughts about humans in general. Do you consider humans as kind and loving creatures? Or would you classify them as devious entities that cannot be trusted?
- "How would you define life?" – With this question, you will discover your life philosophy.
- "What is your ultimate goal?" – Your response to this question determines the goal that you should achieve in order for you to feel complete. This goal has the greatest influence on your entire life.

Chapter 4: Third Hack – Write Down Your Plans

Effective time managers have excellent planning skills. They accomplish objectives (bothminor and major) using lists. Whenever they encounter a new task, they spend ample time to determine what they must do. Then, they map out the process: they write down the steps they need to take to complete the task.

Keep in mind that the time you spend on planning lets you save time in doing the actual activity. It would be wasteful to start doing an activity without any plan: you might end up wasting energy on things that aren't connected to your goal. If you want to manage your time well, you must allocate sufficient time for the planning phase.

Analyze the new activity and list down all of the things that it requires. Don't stop until you feel that you have listed all of the activity's requirements. Once done, you may organize the items in the following ways:

- By priority – This approach relies on the 80/20 principle. According to this principle, 20% of your activities form 80% of the total value of all the activities. Thus, 80% of the things you

need to do are not that important. When using this approach, you won't consider the proper sequence of the activities. Rather, you'll just complete the activities starting from the most important ones.
- By sequence —Arrange the activities starting from the initial phase to the last one. According to time management experts, this chronological approach to arranging objectives is simple and effective.

Consider your plans as flexible tools. They are not cast in stone. You may modify them (or even terminate them) if they are not working as expected. You will make your plans based on the information currently available to you and the assumptions you made regarding your situation. As you perform the activities, you'll learn more about your goal and prove (or refute) your assumptions. These pieces of information will help you improve the effectiveness of your plan.

Important Note: Most failures result from lack of planning. It would be best if you will refrain from taking any action until you have formed a detailed plan.

How to Form a Plan
The following questions will help you form effective plans:
1. What obstacles prevent you from achieving your goal? Why haven't you reached your goal? What is stopping you? Which problems require immediate attention?
2. What skills, data, or knowledge do you need to acquire to complete your project? In most cases, new activities require things that you don't currently have. It is important to identify these missing "pieces" during the planning phase.
    Do you need to get more resources from your boss? Does collecting the missing information require extra time?
3. Are there people, teams, or organizations that you must work with to reach your goal?
4. Which source is the most important? Resources are not created equal – you must determine the crucial ones so you can pay more attention to them. For example, if most of the information that you need belongs to the HR manager, you need to secure his/her cooperation.

Chapter 5: Fourth Hack – Utilize Charts

Most people work in a sequence of different projects. Your success as a professional depends on your capacity to finish projects on time and in the expected quality. Experts consider projects as multitask jobs. Basically, you will only finish a project once you have completed all of the jobs "under" it.

Checklists can help you manage your time and enhance your productivity. They serve as powerful tools that you may utilize to complete more projects. A checklist is a recorded sequence of steps (arranged chronologically) which you prepare before doing the actual work.

The ability to identify the things you must do to reach your goal is crucial in managing your time well. This ability marks excellent thinking.

In this chapter, you will learn how to use a chart called "PERT". PERT charts can help you represent complex projects and tasks in an easy-to-understand format.

How to Generate PERT Charts

The first part of this process requires you to determine your goals. That means you should start by identifying the end result you desire. What is the ideal version of the completed project? Once you have determined the end, start working backwards. This approach will help you list down the things you must do to reach your objective.

PERT (i.e. Program Evaluation Review Technique) charts display each logical step of a process. They show you the things you need to do and when to do them. Because of their effectiveness, countless companies and business executives use PERT charts to attain great performance.

Write down your goal and its completion date. Then, specify the jobs (and their own deadlines) that it requires. Work backwards until you reach the first step of the process. Connect these jobs using lines.

Using this technique, you will be able to control the process completely. You will also have a clear "path" that you can "run" on while working on the project. The "sub-jobs" serve as milestones: they help you determine whether you are making progress or not. Additionally, since the goal and its "sub-jobs" come with specific deadlines, you will have an easier time following your own schedule.

Important Note: Some things will go wrong as you work on a project. Some problems will arise, no matter how hard you try to prevent them. Thus, it is important that you set some "cushion" in your schedule in case delays or failures occur. Effective time managers know how to accept and prepare for potential problems in their projects.

Make Sure That Your People's Goals Are Clear

In some cases, positive intentions and excellent conversations are not enough to accomplish your goals. Leaders (e.g. managers), in particular, need to assign clear objectives for each of their subordinates. As a leader, your performance largely depends on that of your people. Thus, you can greatly benefit from improving the productivity and time management skills of the people working under you.

The best way to help your subordinates grow is by giving them SMART (i.e. specific, measurable, attainable, realistic, and time-bounded) goals. The "measureable" aspect is clearly important. As Peter Drucker, known as the father of modern management, claimed: if you can measure it, you can do it.

Giving deadlines and SMART goals to subordinates is an important aspect of a leader's time management system. You must always set aside time for this task.

Important Note: Assign a deadline to each activity. Activities without deadlines are next to useless. They encourage people to procrastinate.

Chapter 6: Fifth Hack – Create To-Do Lists

Many people praise the effectiveness of to-do lists in managing a person's time. This kind of list serves as a map for all of the activities that you must do within a specific timeframe.

Before you go to sleep, you should write down the tasks that you need to complete for the next day. This approach lets your brain work on those tasks as you sleep. Once you wake up, you will likely have ideas on how to complete the tasks you listed.

Better Sleep
People often experience sleep-related problems when they have to do important things the next day. They do their best to memorize the tasks that they should complete, which forces their brain to do some extra work. If you will write down your tasks before you go to bed, you will surely have a great sleep. Your mind will be able to relax completely, knowing that you have already listed the cannot-be-forgotten tasks for tomorrow on paper.

On average, creating a to-do list consumes twelve minutes. This small investment can help you reap at least two hours of productive work. Thus, you should create to-do lists on a daily basis.

Creating Your Own To-Do List

Consequences play a huge role in managing your time. You can determine the importance of a task by analyzing the consequences of performing it and not performing it. Apply this technique on all of your tasks, and start with the ones that have the most serious consequences. To do this, you may use a method called "ABCDE".

List down every task that you must complete the next day. Next, write "A", "B", "C", "D" or "E" on every item. Assign "A" to tasks that involve grave consequences. Write "B" on tasks that have mild consequences. These tasks are important, but not as crucial as the "A" ones. You must write "C" on the tasks that would be "nice" to complete but don't have any consequences. The letter "D" marks tasks that you may delegate to other people. Lastly, place "E" on the tasks that you must remove from your schedule.

As a general rule, you must delegate a "D" task to other people who can perform them with at least 80% of your own efficiency and effectiveness. By assigning tasks to someone else, you will have more time to do the ones you have marked with "A" and "B".

Important Note: You will have an easier time managing your schedule if you will eliminate tasks that you don't need to perform. Useless tasks will only eat your precious time.

Follow Your To-Do List
Do not work on tasks that are not present in your to-do list. Whenever a new project or activity comes up, include it in your to-do list and assign its priority before working on it. If you will not include new activities in your list, and instead perform them as they arise, you won't be able to control your schedule. You might even waste your precious time on unimportant activities.

There are various time management systems that you can use today. You can download a time management app on your smartphone. You may install time management programs onto your computer. If you are "old school", you may use a pen and a notebook to plan your day. It doesn't matter which medium you will use, as long as you can view or edit its contents quickly and easily.

Chapter 7: Sixth Hack – Identify the Tasks That You Need to Do Now

The following question will help you become an effective time manager:

"What are the things that I can do to maximize my time now?"

That question alone will help you manage your time well. It forces you to determine the most important tasks and their urgency. You can use this question as the core of your own time management system. Many people have tried, and they have reaped astonishing results.

You may consider yourself as a "money-making device". Whenever you perform a task, you create a value for yourself (if you are self-employed) or for the company you are working for. Tasks are not created equal: some are more valuable than others. To become an efficient "money-maker", you need to focus on the activities that offer the highest value to you and/or your employer.

Using the Question as a Lifestyle Guide
The question given above is not limited to job-related tasks. You may also use it in other areas of your life. In some cases, you can get the most out of your time by going home early. Sometimes, you can maximize your time by talking with your loved ones. It is also possible that you can maximize your schedule by maintaining your health (e.g. by exercising regularly).

It doesn't matter what kind of activity you've come up with. If you think it will help you maximize the time currently available to you, do it.

The Four Quadrants
Here's another cool technique that you can use to categorize your tasks:
1. List down all of the tasks that you need to do.
2. Get another piece of paper and divide it into four quadrants. You can do this by drawing a pair of intersecting lines: one vertical and one horizontal.
3. Mark the quadrants as "First", "Second", "Third", and "Fourth".
4. Write down each task on the quadrant that matches the former's urgency and importance. Read the paragraphs given below for more information.

The First Quadrant

This is the quadrant for important and urgent tasks. Basically, important tasks are things that have long-term effects on your life and/or career. Urgent tasks, on the other hand, are things that you cannot delay. Thus, important and urgent tasks require your immediate attention. You need to do them as soon as possible if you want to keep your job or business.

The Second Quadrant

Use this quadrant for important tasks that are not urgent. These are crucial tasks that you may delay for the moment. A great example for this would be a financial report that you must pass four weeks from now. Your job might depend on this report, but (depending on your skills) you may not work on it until the last week.

The Third Quadrant

In this quadrant, you'll list the urgent but unimportant tasks. These tasks require your immediate attention, although they don't add much value to your job or business.

You have to be careful when dealing with this quadrant. In most cases, it will contain numerous tasks that can fill your entire schedule. This quadrant might fool you into thinking that you are busy doing productive stuff. However, you are actually wasting your time on things that don't help you attain significant improvement.

The Fourth Quadrant
This quadrant will hold the unimportant and non-urgent tasks. These tasks are extremely wasteful: they force you to squander your precious time. They don't add anything to your job (and your life). Reading spam emails is an excellent example of this kind of task.

Chapter 8: Seventh Hack – Practice "Single Handling"

"Single handling" is a vital aspect of any time management system. This skill, which is the opposite of multitasking, lets you concentrate on a task. It helps you avoid distractions and wasteful switches between different activities. If you want to manage your time successfully, you must know how to "single handle" activities.

You can be creative, intelligent, or highly skilled, but you won't succeed if you can't concentrate on a task until it is completed. If you don't have the discipline to work on things one at a time, you will keep on wasting your energy and ruining your schedule.

Important Note: Assign sufficient time to each important task. Determine the time it requires and add about 30% more time as a buffer. This way, you can easily adjust to unexpected interruptions. Allotting extra time in completing a task is one of the most powerful techniques that you can use.

More Information about Single Handling

With this technique, you will keep on performing a single task until you complete it.

Single handling relies on discipline: it stops you from switching between different tasks.

You can apply this technique on emails. Delete unimportant messages as soon as possible and work on the important ones (e.g. by replying to the senders). Don't exit your email account or email program (e.g. Thunderbird) until you have dealt with all of those messages.

Single handling is a time management technique that can help you boost productivity. According to recent studies, you will lose rhythm and momentum if you will stop doing an activity to do another one. Once you need to work on the first task again, you must spend some time reviewing the activity and remembering where you "left" off. Reviewing and remembering stuff can consume the time that you could spend on more productive tasks.

Do Not Multitask
Many people are praising the benefits of multitasking. These individuals claim that they can perform different tasks simultaneously without sacrificing their effectiveness and efficiency. Unfortunately, studies have proved that this idea is completely false.

Researchers discovered that multitasking is more of "task-switching". Here's a basic truth: no one can perform two or more things at the same time. You need to stop performing an activity before you can do the next one. You will transfer your energy and focus from the first task to the second task.

Before you can work on the first task again, you must perform another transfer of focus and energy. Here's an interesting fact: the "transfer process" itself is extremely tiring.

Important Note: You probably think that you can save time by doing two or more tasks at the same time. However, multitasking can make you waste your time quickly. Multitasking is an approach that burns your energy and concentration. In fact, some researchers claim that multitasking has negative effects on a person's intelligence. If you don't want to become stupid, work on your tasks one at a time.

Chapter 9: Eighth Hack – Beat Procrastination

People claim that procrastination steals time. This "sin" prevents people from completing their jobs on schedule. Your ability to beat procrastination spells the difference between growth and stagnation in your professional life.

You should know that everyone procrastinates. Each individual has limited time and countless things to do. If every person procrastinates, what separates productive individuals from unproductive ones?

Well, productive people procrastinate on unimportant activities. Unproductive people procrastinate on activities that have a huge impact on their professional (and sometimes personal) life. To become an effective time manager, you must practice creative procrastination.

Here are some techniques that you can use to beat procrastination:

Mind Programming
Program your mind to do important tasks as soon as possible. The following two-word combo can help you with this:

"Do it!"

Say these words whenever you feel like you are procrastinating on a job. Tell yourself to "Do it! Do it! Do it!" Repeat these words with energy.

According to experts, these two words can help you achieve a quick but significant improvement in your productivity.

Bite-Size Pieces Approach
In most cases, the best way to perform a task is by dividing it into various bite-size pieces. This approach helps you gain more control over your time and the project itself.

Divide the task into small subtasks and record them. It would be best if you'll arrange the subtasks in chronological order. Force yourself to complete the first task before moving on to the second one. This way, you will be able to complete the project without skipping any step.

Salami Slice Approach

This approach is similar to the previous one. The main difference between these approaches is that "salami slice" doesn't concentrate on how you arrange the steps. Rather, it simply requires you to perform one of the subtasks at a time.

When using this approach, just divide the task into multiple subtasks. Then, work on the subtasks one by one. Since you don't have to start from any particular step, you can begin the task by conducting the subtask you are most comfortable with.

Chapter 10: Ninth Hack – Manage Interruptions

Experts consider interruptions as huge time wasters. Interruptions can make you lose your momentum and force you to switch between different tasks. An interruption can take simple forms, such as a "text" message from a friend, unexpected visitors who want to talk to you, or computer crashes.

According to recent studies, however, the worst interruptions involve other human beings. For example, employees spend a significant portion of their time in the office chatting with their coworkers. Some employees even start chatting with others as soon as they enter the office. Then, they continue the idle chat for the next one to two hours.

Here are some techniques that you can use to control interruptions:

Work When You Need to Work
You must work when it is time for you to work. When you are in the office, start working as soon as possible. Do not engage in idle conversations, read a magazine, or watch cat videos online. There are things you need to

do. It would be best if you will start doing those things immediately.

Minimize all of the Interruptions
It's impossible to prevent all forms of interruptions. Whenever you face an interruption, try to minimize its effects by going back to your work quickly. If someone calls you, for example, don't waste time with pleasantries. Here's a format that you can use:

"Hi (insert name here). How can I help you?"

Never beat around the bush. Doing so will lead to wasted minutes (or even hours). If you need to call someone, you must write down the things you want to talk about. This approach lets you cover all of the important points of the conversation quickly. Your list will also serve as a useful guideline for your call. If the conversation heads to a topic you didn't write down, you may apologize and go back to the important topics or end the call (i.e. if you have covered all of the points you listed).

Ask Other People
Other people are wasting your time. However, you cannot deny the fact that you also waste their time. It would be great if you'll ask them about the things you do that affect their

schedule negatively. This kind of conversation often leads to a win-win situation for the parties involved. Your coworkers can specify the things that affect their productivity negatively. Meanwhile, you will gain more information about the interruptions present in your workplace. Once you know how you waste other people's time, you will have better chances of managing your own time successfully.

Chapter 11: Tenth Hack - Control the Phone

Telephones can either help you or enslave you. You become a "phone slave" if you think you must answer the telephone whenever it rings. To manage your time successfully, you need to control your phone well.

There are two techniques that you can use to manage your phone. These techniques are:
- Ask someone to screen your calls – This technique works best for people who have assistants or secretaries.
- Make sure that your phone is "silent" – With this technique, you'll rely on your voicemail. The main disadvantage of this technique is that it may cause you to miss urgent calls.

In general, people become "phone slaves" because of curiosity. They wonder who the caller is or what the call is about. This curiosity becomes so strong the "victims" cannot help but to press the "Answer" button.

When you are in an important meeting, turn off your phone and minimize interruptions. Often, callers can wait until the person they need becomes available.

Call People in Batches

If you should call people throughout the day, make your phone calls in a specific part of your schedule. Allot a period of time in which you will focus on your calls and ignore other tasks. Before starting your "phone time", you must list down the names of the people you need to call. Specify the phone number of each person as well as the reason for the conversation.

Your scheduled phone calls are as important as your scheduled meetings. Before making a top priority call, it would be best if you will write down your agenda for that conversation. It would be a huge waste of your time if you will call an individual and forget what you want to talk about.

Chapter 12: Eleventh Hack – Plan Your Meetings Well

Professionals spend about 25% to 50% of their time in meetings. These meetings come in different types: one-on-one, quick "hallway meetings", or sit-down conversations in the office. However, about 50% of the time spent on meetings goes to waste. A meeting can consume your precious time without producing significant value. If you want to succeed as a professional, you should know how to use meetings effectively.

Check the Costs
Each meeting should have a good reason behind it. Treat meetings as business investments: they require time, people, place, and other types of resources. Considering that you are using various resources for each meeting, you have to make sure that you will get sufficient ROI (i.e. return on investment) from it.

Important Note: Never go to unnecessary meetings. Check the importance of a meeting before attending. If you don't need to attend, don't attend. If you are the organizer, limit your invitations to people that are needed in the meeting.

Specify the Meeting's Agenda

You should prepare the agenda of each meeting you will organize. Analyze the items you included in the meeting's agenda and focus on the crucial ones first. Make sure that the meeting follows the agenda you prepared. As the leader of the meeting, you must keep the conversation on the right track. In addition, you need to complete every item before discussing the next one.

Chapter 13: Twelfth Hack – Learn How to Read Fast

You read stories, reports, news articles, emails, and work-related information on a daily basis. These reading materials contain a lot of words that you must take in. Thus, you spend minutes (or even hours) just reading numerous words. If you want to manage your time well, you should improve your reading skills. You are now living in a world that depends on knowledge and information – the ability to read fast can help you greatly.

Since your time is finite, you should carefully choose the things you read. The last thing you want to do is spend your precious time reading unimportant materials. If you want to save more of your reading time, use your keyboard's Delete key often.

Master the Art of "Speed Reading"
"Speed reading" is a skill that lets you read hundreds of words quickly without sacrificing comprehension. With this technique, you'll be able to understand several pages of critical information quickly and easily. Thus, you will have an easier time managing your schedule.

There are lots of books and online articles related to speed reading. You can get a good guide just by running a Google search.

Collect Important Reading Materials
You will encounter interesting and/or important reading materials as you go through your scheduled activities. Instead of perusing the materials right then and there, you can just collect them in a certain folder. This approach helps you in following your schedule and completing your tasks on time. Obviously, spending time on articles you'll find out of nowhere can ruin your time management system.

Collecting reading materials and perusing them at a later time also help you in improving your focus. Stopping an activity to read an interesting article involves "task-shifting". You won't be able to focus on the activity you are currently doing. Since you are in the middle of doing something, focusing on the article is extremely difficult.

Don't Read Unimportant Stuff
You can save your time by ignoring unnecessary reading materials. It would be best if you will screen reading materials before you invest your time on them. For example, you can determine the relevance and/or

importance of a book by checking its introduction and table of contents. You may also get more data regarding the author.

If you're not satisfied with the data you have gathered regarding the material, don't read it.

Chapter 14: Thirteenth Hack – Keep Your Workspace Organized

An organized workspace can boost your productivity and save your time. If your workspace is clean, you can quickly find anything you need. You can also complete your tasks without going through mountains of unrelated stuff.

Time managers make sure that their workspace is clean. They ensure that each object on their table is related to the task they are currently working on. This way, they can prevent confusion and distraction. Thus, they complete their tasks quickly and efficiently.

Here's a simple technique that you can use:
Separate your files (both "online" and "offline") into different categories. Concentrate on your current activity. If the situation permits, limit the number of items that you'll use for the task.

Important Note: Make sure that you have everything you need to finish your tasks. Make the necessary preparations before doing the activity itself. Stopping an activity in order to get something can ruin your momentum.

Organization and Productivity

Some individuals claim that they become more productive when working in a messy environment. Recent studies, however, have debunked this myth. When "messy people" (i.e. individuals who "thrive" in cluttered places) were asked to clean their desks, they experienced a 100% to 200% increase in productivity.

If your desk is cluttered, you will surely spend some time looking for the things you need. In addition, the clutter has a psychological effect —it makes you think that you can't organize stuff. This subconscious belief drags your productivity down and stops you from focusing on your task.

Conclusion

Thank you again for purchasing this book!

I hope this book was able to help you become a skilled time manager.

The next step is to continue creating to-do lists and categorizing your tasks. With continuous practice, you will be able to manage your time effortlessly. Keep these hacks in mind – they will help you reach topnotch performance.

Finally, if you enjoyed this book, then I'd like to ask you for a favor, would you be kind enough to leave a review for this book on Amazon? It'd be greatly appreciated!

Thank you and good luck!

www.ingramcontent.com/pod-product-compliance
Lightning Source LLC
Chambersburg PA
CBHW070411190526
45169CB00003B/1203